D0772838

The *The* **HUMAN BODY**

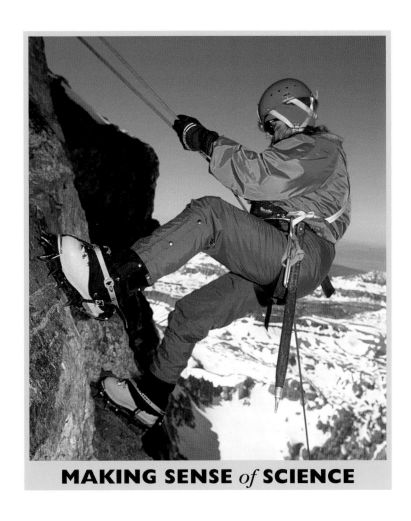

MAKING SENSE *of* SCIENCE

Peter Riley

Smart Apple Media

WHITE MOUNTAIN LIBRARY
SWEETWATER COUNTY LIBRARY SYSTEM
ROCK SPRINGS, WYOMING

First published in 2004 by Franklin Watts
96 Leonard Street, London EC2A 4XD

Franklin Watts Australia
45–51 Huntley Street, Alexandria NSW 2015

This edition published under license from Franklin Watts. All rights reserved.
Text copyright © 2004 Peter Riley.
Design and concept © 2004 Franklin Watts.

Series editor: Rachel Cooke, Editor: Kate Newport,
Art director: Jonathan Hair, Designer: Mo Choy

Picture credits:
AJ Photo/SPL: 13b.
Ancient Art & Architecture Collection/Topham: 17b.
Bettmann/Corbis: 9t, 11c. BSIP, Laurent/SPL: 29cl.
Dr. Jeremy Burgess/SPL: 15b. CC Studio/SPL: 28b.
Pr S.Cinti/CNRI /SPL: 6bl. CNRI/SPL: 7br.
Adam Hart-Davis/SPL: 7cl, 7bl.
Pascal Goetgheluck/SPL: 29tr.
Sally Greenhill/S & R Greenhill: 20, 21.
Image Works/Topham: 25t. Coneyl Jay/SPL: 28c.
Nancy Kedersha /UCLA /SPL: 19bl.
Dr. Kari Lounatmaa/SPL: front cover inset.
Moredun Scientific Ltd/SPL: 25b. Dr. G. Moscoso/SPL: 23c.
Prof. P. Motta/Dept. of Anatomy /University "La Sapienza," Rome/SPL: 6br.
Chris Priest & Mark Clarke/SPL: 27t.
J.C. Revy/SPL: 11b. Galen Rowell/Corbis: front cover main.
Sovereign, ISM/SPL: 5. SPL: 17bl, 27b.
Dr. Linda Stannard, UCT/SPL: 24t, 24c.
VVG/SPL: 16cr.

All other photography by Ray Moller.

Published in the United States by Smart Apple Media
2140 Howard Drive West, North Mankato, Minnesota 56003

U.S. publication copyright © 2006 Smart Apple Media
International copyright reserved in all countries. No part of this book may be reproduced
in any form without written permission from the publisher.
Printed in the United States of America

Library of Congress Cataloging-in-Publication Data

Riley, Peter D.
The human body / by Peter Riley.
p. cm. — (Making sense of science)
Includes index.
ISBN 1-58340-717-0
1. Human physiology—Juvenile literature. 2. Body, Human—Juvenile literature. I. Title.

QP37.R554 2005
612—dc22   2004059967

2 4 6 8 9 7 5 3 1

CONTENTS

WHAT HAPPENS INSIDE THE BODY?

Stand or sit still—you might say that you are "doing nothing." But under the skin, your body is always busy. The heart pumps blood around the body, the skeleton supports you, and the muscles work with the senses to keep you balanced. The lungs take in fresh air and push old air out. The digestive system breaks down food so you can get nutrients from it.

The body is made up of many different organs, each with a different task. The organs work together in groups called organ systems. There are 11 organ systems.

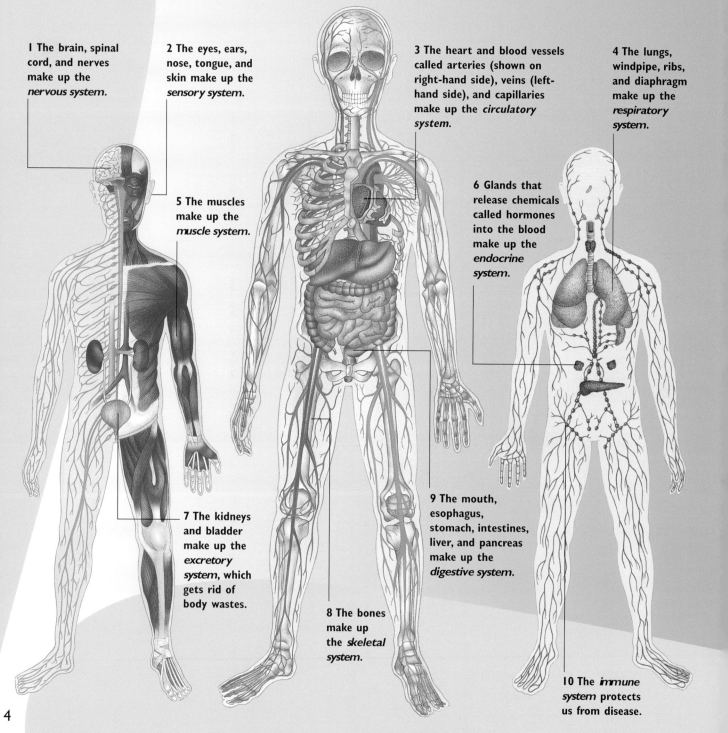

1 The brain, spinal cord, and nerves make up the *nervous system*.

2 The eyes, ears, nose, tongue, and skin make up the *sensory system*.

3 The heart and blood vessels called arteries (shown on right-hand side), veins (left-hand side), and capillaries make up the *circulatory system*.

4 The lungs, windpipe, ribs, and diaphragm make up the *respiratory system*.

5 The muscles make up the *muscle system*.

6 Glands that release chemicals called hormones into the blood make up the *endocrine system*.

7 The kidneys and bladder make up the *excretory system*, which gets rid of body wastes.

8 The bones make up the *skeletal system*.

9 The mouth, esophagus, stomach, intestines, liver, and pancreas make up the *digestive system*.

10 The *immune system* protects us from disease.

ovaries

II The ovaries in the female and the testicles in the male make up the *reproductive system*.

testicles

HOW HEAVY ARE YOUR BONES AND MUSCLES?

Figure out the mass (weight) of your bones and muscles. Bones make up 15 percent of your body mass, and muscles make up about 45 percent. Weigh yourself and find your mass. Now figure out the mass of your bones and muscles as follows:

• Total mass = bone mass
(e.g. 90 pounds/41 kg) x 15/100 = (e.g. 13.5 pounds/6.1 kg).

• Total mass = muscle mass
(e.g. 90 pounds/41 kg) x 45/100 = (e.g. 40.5 pounds/18.4 kg)

CLAUDIUS GALEN

Galen (c. A.D. 129–216) was a Greek doctor who was interested in how the insides of the body were arranged. At that time, it was forbidden to cut up human bodies, so he cut up the bodies of apes and other animals instead. He supposed that the human body was arranged in a similar way to these animals, but some of his ideas were later shown to be untrue.

This scan of the head shows the position of the brain. The folded part across the top is called the cerebrum. It has many functions. You are using yours right now to understand the picture.

LOOKING INSIDE THE BODY

Scientists and doctors have worked together for hundreds of years to learn about the body and how it works. An important part of this knowledge has come from dissecting (cutting open) dead bodies. The knowledge gained from dissections has made it possible for surgeons to operate safely on living people.

Today we have ways of looking inside the body without cutting it open. X rays, for instance, pass through most body organs but are stopped by bones and teeth. By photographing the body with X rays, it is possible to see the bones or teeth inside the flesh.

Machines called scanners can take a detailed picture through the body using either X rays or magnetism and radio waves. Doctors can use such scans to help diagnose a patient's illness.

THE BODY'S BUILDING BLOCKS

The human body is made of tiny packets of life called cells. About 200 cells would fit into the period at the end of this sentence, and the human body contains up to 65 billion of them.

There are many different kinds of cells in the body, but they all have the same three basic features: a nucleus, cytoplasm, and a cell membrane.

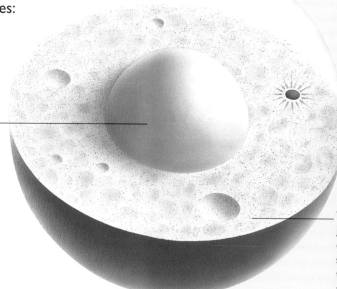

The *cell membrane* holds in the cytoplasm and the nucleus. There are tiny holes in it called pores. They control the movement of substances into and out of the cell.

The *nucleus* is the control center of the cell. It contains all the information that the cell needs to grow properly and carry out its tasks.

The *cytoplasm* is a thin jelly-like substance. It contains a variety of tiny structures that work together to keep the cell alive.

DIFFERENT TYPES OF CELLS

Certain cells are designed to perform particular tasks. For example, muscle cells are long and thin. They contain tiny threads that can slide over each other to make the cell contract, or get shorter. Because muscles are made from many muscle cells, when the muscle cells shorten, the whole muscle contracts and causes movement.

Another kind of cell lines your windpipe. These cells have tiny hairs called cilia, which can wave back and forth. The cilia are covered in a layer of sticky mucus, which traps dust from the air. The waving action of the cilia moves the dust and mucus to the back of your mouth, where you swallow it.

Smooth muscle cells are long. They are wider in the center and thinner toward each end.

These are cells that line and protect the windpipe. They are covered with tiny hairs called cilia.

WATCH YOUR IRIS SHRINK

The iris of the eye is made of long, thin muscle cells. Muscles running in a ring around the iris can contract to shrink the pupil and let less light into the eye. Muscles that radiate out like spokes in a wheel can contract to open the pupil and let in more light.

Set a lamp by a mirror, then cover your eyes with your hand for two minutes. Now open your eyes and look in the mirror. What happens to the pupils?

iris   pupil

The pupils contract when you open your eyes so that too much light does not reach the sensitive retina at the back of the eye.

CELLS, TISSUES, AND ORGANS

In the same way that many muscle cells are organized together into muscles, other kinds of cells do not work alone but combine together in large numbers to form tissues. Muscles are one kind of tissue. Another is epithelium—cells that cover a surface, such as the cells lining the windpipe.

Groups of tissues develop next to each other to form organs. For example, the stomach contains tissues that produce digestive juices and muscular tissues that churn up the food.

Most human body cells are colorless, which makes them difficult to see under a microscope. In 1856, an English chemist named **William Perkin (1838–1907)** discovered that dyes could be made from substances in coal tar. Other scientists, such as German **Paul Ehrlich (1854–1915)**, began experimenting with the dyes and found that they could be used to stain the different parts of a cell and make them easier to see.

CANCERS

Cancers are caused by cells that have something wrong with the nucleus, making them grow uncontrollably. This forms a lump called a tumor. If a patient is found to have a lump that might be cancerous, cells may be taken from it and examined under a microscope to see if they are cancer cells.

Cancer cells have a different appearance than normal cells and can be identified by examining tissues with a microscope.

HOW DO WE KEEP GOING?

Food provides the body with important substances called nutrients. The body uses nutrients to make the materials needed for new cells. Nutrients also provide the energy needed to keep cells alive. There are six groups of nutrients.

fat

protein and fat

protein and carbohydrates

fiber, carbohydrates, and vitamins

fiber, protein, and minerals

protein, minerals, and fat

1. PROTEINS

Proteins provide materials for making and repairing cells and are needed for growth. They also make hormones (see pages 20 and 21) and enzymes (see page 10). Meat, fish, peas, beans, cereals, cheese, and milk are all rich in protein.

2. FATS

Fats provide materials for making cell membranes and an insulating layer under the skin to help keep the body warm. They also provide energy. Meat, nuts, hard cheese, and cream are all rich in fat.

TEST FOR FAT

Gather together different foods. Rub each one on a piece of white paper, then set the paper aside to allow any water to dry. Hold the paper up to a window or light. If you can see light through the rub mark, the food contains fat.

3. CARBOHYDRATES

Carbohydrates provide energy. Sugars are simple types of carbohydrates. Foods such as rice, pasta, bread, potatoes, and fruit are also rich in carbohydrates.

4. MINERALS

Minerals are needed for many functions in the body. Iron is needed to make red blood cells, and calcium is needed to make bone and help muscles work. Meat, eggs, milk, cheese, spinach, and green vegetables are all mineral-rich foods.

5. VITAMINS

Vitamins help the body grow properly and protect it from disease. Foods rich in vitamins include carrots, tomatoes, milk, butter, oranges, potatoes, and cabbage.

6. FIBER

Fiber helps muscles in the stomach and intestines push food through the digestive system and prevents constipation. Fiber is found in foods such as cereals, cabbage, beans, and peas.

FINDING THE NUTRIENTS

Look at your supper and decide which foods are rich in each of the six different kinds of nutrients. Is your meal providing them all?

James Lind first worked as a surgeon's mate in the British navy when he became a doctor. He went on to run a navy hospital and proved that scurvy was due to a poor diet.

In the 18th century, a disease called scurvy was common among sailors. The disease causes blood vessels to break down and causes bleeding in the gums, joints, and inside the body. In some cases, it can result in death. A Scottish doctor named James Lind (1716–1794) believed that scurvy was common in sailors because of their diet of meat broth, porridge, and biscuits. When he tried adding other foods to the diet, he found that citrus fruits such as limes and lemons prevented scurvy. Today we know that these fruits contain vitamin C, which is needed to keep blood vessels healthy.

THE **FOOD PYRAMID**

We do not need the same amount of all the nutrients. For example, we need only a small amount of fat—eating too much is unhealthy. An easy way to remember the quantities of nutrients to eat is to use a food pyramid like the one shown here. We need only small amounts of foods at the top of the pyramid, but large amounts of foods at the base of the pyramid.

BREAKING DOWN FOOD

The nutrients in food cannot pass directly to the cells where they are needed. Our bodies must first digest the food (break it down) to release the nutrients. Then the nutrients must pass out of the digestive system and into the blood, which carries them to the cells.

Digestion takes place in the digestive system—your gut, or alimentary canal. Take a trip along the alimentary canal by following the numbered captions in this picture.

1 Food enters through the *mouth* and is chewed into small pieces by the teeth. Saliva produced in the mouth starts breaking down carbohydrates in the food.

2 Taste buds on the *tongue* help us taste the food. The tongue then pushes the food to the back of the mouth.

3 Muscles produce a wave of movement along the *esophagus* that pushes food into the stomach.

4 The *stomach* releases acid to kill germs and starts to break down protein. The stomach also churns the food to mix it up.

liver

5 In the *duodenum*, the gall bladder releases bile onto the food. The bile breaks up fat into tiny droplets.

6 The *pancreas* releases enzymes that break down proteins, fats, and carbohydrates so that they dissolve.

7 In the *small intestine*, all the nutrients pass through the intestine wall and into the blood.

8 In the *large intestine*, water is taken back into the blood to be used again to make saliva and other juices.

9 The *rectum* stores undigested food such as fiber and releases it through the anus.

BILE IN ACTION

The bile released from the duodenum breaks fats in the food into tiny droplets, which are easier to digest. You can see how this works using liquid handsoap. Put a few drops of cooking oil in a glass of water and stir it up. How big are the fat drops? Now add a few drops of liquid soap and stir again. How big are the drops now?

TESTING DIGESTION

After Alexis St. Martin was shot in the stomach, he recovered to full health except for a hole in his stomach. This helped William Beaumont make discoveries about digestion.

William Beaumont (1785–1853), an American surgeon, saved the life of Alexis St. Martin, who had been shot in the stomach. At the end of the operation, Beaumont was unable to close the wound completely, and a hole was left in the stomach. Beaumont carried out several experiments in which he put samples of food on strings into St. Martin's stomach and pulled them out later to see how the stomach had changed them. He found, for instance, that vegetables took longer to digest than meat, and that the stomach juices needed to be warm to break down food.

LOOKING AT DIGESTION

Barium is a metal that can take part in many chemical reactions to make a range of compounds. One compound, called barium sulphate, is particularly useful, as it can move harmlessly through the alimentary canal yet stops X rays. This makes it possible to look at the alimentary canal. A patient eats a meal of barium sulphate (called a barium meal) before the alimentary canal is X-rayed.

This X ray shows the stomach after a barium meal.

BREATHING FOR ENERGY

People tend to think of respiration as breathing, but it is really something else. Breathing is the changing of gases in the lungs. Respiration is the release of energy from food, and it takes place in every cell in the body. Every minute of the day, our lungs need to take in fresh air and push out stale air. Our lungs are moving oxygen into the body and carbon dioxide out. The blood then carries these gases between the lungs and the cells.

1 We breathe air in and out through the nose. The nasal passages filter dust from incoming air and warm and moisten the air. Dust, dry air, and cold air can all damage lung tissues.

2 Rings of stiff cartilage in the windpipe keep it open all the time. Cells with tiny hairs (cilia) move dust away from the lungs to be swallowed (see page 6).

3 The windpipe divides into two bronchi (air tubes), one going to each lung.

4 If you look closely at the lungs, you can see how the bronchi divide many times to form millions of tiny air tubes. At the end of each tube is an air pocket.

6 The diaphragm separates the chest from the abdomen. It moves up and down in a pumping action to change the air in the lungs.

5 If you look closer still, you can see the blood flowing in the walls of the air pockets. It picks up oxygen from the air and takes it to the cells. The blood also releases waste carbon dioxide into the lungs. The millions of air pockets enable these gases to enter and leave the body very quickly.

blood vessels

air pockets

LUNG SURFACE AREA

If the lungs could be unfolded, they would cover an area the size of a tennis court. A tissue is about 800 times smaller than the area of the lungs. Try crumpling a tissue into as small a ball as possible. If you can pack it tight enough to fit on a tablespoon, the tissue will be as tightly packed as the tissues in the lungs (a tablespoon is about 800 times smaller than the space in your chest).

CHANGING THE AIR

The pumping action of the respiratory system is called ventilation. Raising the ribs and lowering the diaphragm expands the lungs and pulls air into them.

Lowering the ribs and raising the diaphragm pushes air out of the lungs.

When early scientists made their dissections, they did not always understand what they saw. Galen, for example, believed that there was a life spirit in the air. He thought that when air was breathed in, it passed into the windpipe, then into a vein close to the heart, and then into the heart itself. From there the life spirit traveled in the blood to the brain and then changed into an animal spirit, which moved down the nerves and made the body move.

This is an early statue of Galen. He was one of the first thinkers to use dissections to test his ideas.

LUNG DISEASE

Scientists don't always do experiments to draw conclusions. Sometimes they just collect data and

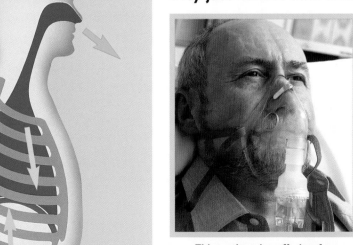

This patient is suffering from a disease brought on by smoking. He is using special equipment to help him breathe.

study it. The link between smoking and lung disease was discovered this way. When data was collected about people who died from lung disease, it was found that many of them had been smokers. Further studies showed that most people who died of lung cancer were also smokers. The link between smoking and cancer was finally made when experiments were done on tobacco smoke. They showed that there were chemicals in the smoke that caused cancer.

13

THE HEART AND BLOOD

The circulatory system is made up of the heart, the blood vessels, and the blood itself. Blood is the body's transport system. It carries essential substances to the cells and takes away their wastes. The pumping action of the heart moves the blood around the body.

It takes about 45 seconds for the blood to make one complete circuit of the circulatory system.

THE HEART

Your heart is a bag of muscle about the size of your fist. The muscle is called cardiac muscle and contracts regularly throughout your life. The heart is basically two pumps side by side. Each pump has two valves, which let the blood move through them one way but not the other. As the pumps work, the valves open and close, making the sounds we call heartbeats.

The heart has four chambers, two to each pump.

The right side of the heart collects blood from the body and pushes it to the lungs, where it collects oxygen.

The left side of the heart receives blood from the lungs and pushes it around the body.

head
heart

right lung

left lung

liver

intestines

kidneys

legs

The pumping of the blood makes the blood vessels throughout the body expand and contract. This can be felt as a throbbing movement we call the pulse. The pulse throbs at the same rate as the heart beats and can be used to tell how fast the heart is beating.

14

TAKE YOUR PULSE

Hold out your right hand with the palm up. Put your left thumb under your right wrist and use two fingers of your left hand to feel the top of your right wrist. When you press down, you will feel the throbbing of the pulse.

Count the number of times your pulse throbs in 15 seconds and multiply by four to find how fast the heart is beating in a minute. Run around for two minutes, then take your pulse again. How has it changed?

MOVING SUBSTANCES AROUND

The blood carries oxygen from the lungs, and nutrients from the small intestine, to all the body's cells. It takes away their wastes, too. One waste product is carbon dioxide, which the blood takes to the lungs. Another is a substance called urea, which is produced by cells in the liver as they break down protein that the body does not need. The urea is carried in the blood to the kidneys, where it forms part of your urine.

WHAT **MAKES** THE **BLOOD MOVE?**

Until the 17th century no one understood how the circulation system worked. William Harvey (1578–1657) was one of the royal physicians (doctors) to Kings James I and Charles I of England. He spent many years studying the circulation of animals. In 1628, he published a famous book, *On the Motion of the Heart and Blood in Animals,* in which he showed that the heart acted as a pump to move the blood around the body.

This woodcut by Harvey shows the valves in the veins of the forearm. On the left, for example, the finger has been passed along the vein from O to H (away from the heart).

BONES AND MUSCLES

Your bones join together to make the skeleton—the body's "scaffolding." The skeleton is a framework for the muscles, which provide the power of movement. However, two types of muscles are not attached to bone. They are smooth muscles, like those in the iris (see page 7), and cardiac muscles (see page 14).

skull

shoulder joint

ribcage

arm bones

spine

vertebrae

pelvis

hip joint

leg bones

kneecap

LIVING BONES

We tend to think of bones as lifeless, because we usually see them only in skeletons. But our bones contain living cells. Some of these cells use substances from our food, such as calcium, to make the hard material we call bone. The center of some bones contains bone marrow, where blood cells are produced.

These are bone cells viewed under a microscope. They become surrounded by the bony material they produce.

HOW BONES HELP

The skeleton supports all the soft parts of the body. If the bones were not present, the organs would squash each other and stop working. Bones also provide extra protection for important organs. For example, the brain is enclosed in the bones of the skull, and the heart and lungs are protected by the ribcage.

JOINED BY JOINTS

Bones are not all rigidly attached, but have joints that allow movement. Joints such as the hip and shoulder can move a great deal in many directions. Knee and elbow joints can only move back and forth, while joints in the skull and pelvis don't move at all.

OILING THE JOINTS

If the bones in a joint rubbed against each other, they would soon wear down.

cartilage

synovial fluid

So in joints that move a lot, the ends of the bones are capped with tough cartilage and a liquid called synovial fluid. The fluid is produced to oil the joints and reduce friction.

WORKING IN PAIRS

We have seen (page 6) how tiny threads inside muscle cells slide over each other to make the muscles contract (shorten). However, when a muscle relaxes, it cannot lengthen on its own; the threads have to be pulled apart. So muscles are arranged in pairs that work together. One muscle pair is the biceps and triceps in the upper arm.

When the biceps contracts, it stretches and lengthens the triceps.

When the triceps contracts, it stretches the biceps.

The muscles are attached to the bones by tough cords called tendons.

FIND YOUR TENDONS

Your fingers are connected to the muscles that move them by long tendons. Look at the back of your hand and stretch your fingers. You should be able to see or feel the tendons running from the fingers down the back of the hand. Can you find the muscles that these tendons are attached to? Now try feeling for the tendons on the inside of your elbows and at the back of your knees.

Secunda II.

This is an anatomical diagram drawn by Vesalius in the 16th century. It shows the female form.

VESALIUS

Andreas Vesalius (1514–1564) was a Flemish (Belgian) scientist. He lived at a time when the dissection of human bodies was allowed and repeated Galen's animal dissections in humans (see page 5). He found many inaccuracies in Galen's work. Vesalius made dissections of the human body and then drew pictures of them. These beautiful and accurate drawings were used by others who were investigating the human body.

THE BRAIN AND NERVES

Our senses give us information about the world around us. They send information to the brain, which is the control center of the nervous system. The brain may store this information as a memory, process it by comparing it with what the person already knows, or use it to send out messages of its own to other parts of the body.

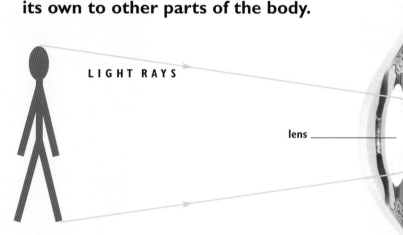

LIGHT RAYS

retina

lens

image

nerves to brain

Different senses are designed to pick up different kinds of information. The eyes, for example, detect light waves, while the ears pick up sound waves. Inside each sense organ, the information is changed into tiny bursts of electricity called nerve impulses, which move along nerves to the brain.

Light from something you see gets bent by the lens to form an image on the retina at the back of the eye. Nerves then carry messages about the picture to the brain.

movement

touch

taste

hearing

thinking

speaking

seeing

Different parts of the brain have different jobs, as shown on this brain map.

RECORDING THE BRAIN

In 1929, German psychiatrist Hans Berger (1873–1941) showed that it was possible to record the electrical activity of the brain on a chart, using electrodes attached to the outside of the skull. He did this with a machine he called an electroencephalograph, or EEG. Today, EEGs are used in hospitals around the world to diagnose brain disorders such as epilepsy.

The brain "makes sense" of the nerve impulses from the various senses. For instance, images sent to the brain from the eyes are upside down, but the brain turns them right side up. If a ball is being thrown to you, the brain quickly sends out messages to the muscles in your arms and hands so you can catch it.

HOW FAST CAN MESSAGES TRAVEL THROUGH YOUR NERVOUS SYSTEM?

Find out how fast electrical messages travel from your eye to your brain and then to your hand. Hold out your hand with your thumb and fingers about 2 inches (5 cm) apart. Ask a friend to hold a ruler above your hand so that the lower end is just between your thumb and fingers. Tell your friend to let go of the ruler at any time. As he or she drops the ruler, try to catch it.

If only a small length of the ruler falls before you catch it, messages have traveled fast from your eye to your brain and hand. If you fail to catch the ruler, the messages have traveled slowly.

connections to other nerves or muscles

cell body

nerve fiber

CELLS OF THE NERVOUS SYSTEM

Nerves are made up of many nerve cells, which have long, thin fibers that carry the nerve impulses. The end of each nerve cell connects to one or more other nerve cells, or to a muscle.

In the brain, each nerve cell is connected to many others. Nerve impulses pass around whole groups of brain cells to help us think and remember things.

THE **EFFECTS** OF **ALCOHOL** AND **DRUGS**

Scientific investigations have shown that drinking large amounts of alcohol or taking drugs can damage the nervous system and cause illnesses. Alcohol, for example, slows down the speed at which the nervous system can send its messages. This makes a person react more slowly to changes around them and increases the risk of them having an accident.

GROWING AND CHANGING

If you look at photographs of people at different ages, you can see how they have grown and changed. We grow as our cells divide to form more cells. How we grow is controlled by chemicals in the body called hormones. What we eat also affects how we grow.

Growth is easy to see—a person increases in height and weight. Growth can also cause changes. As the bones of the skull grow, they cause the face to change. For example, a baby may have a round face, but as the person grows, the shape of the face usually changes from round to oval.

At six months old.

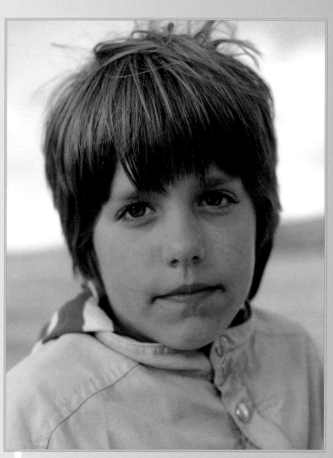

At 10 years old.

CELLS DIVIDING

The body grows by cell division—a single cell divides to make two new ones.

The nucleus of the cell divides first.

Next, a groove develops in the cell membrane.

HOW FAST DOES YOUR THUMBNAIL GROW?

Cut your thumbnail and measure the distance from the base of the nail to the cut edge. A week later, measure again and see how much the nail has grown.

At 20 years old.

The groove deepens and eventually separates the cytoplasm to form two cells.

HORMONES AND GROWTH

Underneath the brain is an organ called the pituitary gland. It makes chemicals called hormones and releases them into the blood through the glands that make up the endocrine system. One hormone is called growth hormone. It passes around the body and makes cells divide and organs grow. When a person reaches the age of about 12, the sex organs—the ovaries in females and the testicles in males—also begin to produce hormones. The hormone produced by the ovaries causes the breasts to develop and the hips to widen. The hormone produced by the testicles makes the voice deepen and causes the testicles and penis to grow bigger.

You can begin to see these changes if you look at photographs of you and your friends and family at different ages. The panel on the left shows the same person at three different stages in her life.

BABY MILK

Babies are normally fed breast milk early in their life. In addition to providing all the food a baby needs, the milk provides antibodies to help protect the baby against disease (see page 26). However, many young babies also drink a synthetic kind of milk sold as a powder. Much research has been done to make sure that this milk gives babies everything they need for healthy growth.

A new human being grows from a single cell called a zygote. Unlike all other cells, a zygote is made when two cells join, rather than by a cell dividing in two. The two cells that combine are a sperm cell from the father and an egg cell from the mother.

The zygote then divides and begins to grow inside its mother, using food and oxygen from her blood. After nine months, a new baby is born.

REPRODUCTIVE ORGANS

Males and females each have special organs for reproduction. Females have two ovaries that produce egg cells. These are connected by tubes (oviducts, or Fallopian tubes) to the womb, which is connected to the outside by a passage called the vagina.

In males, the reproductive organs are two testicles, which produce sperm cells. They are connected by tubes to the prostate gland and the penis.

HOW SEX CELLS MEET

The sex cells (the sperm and egg cells) reach each other in the following way. Sperm cells pass from the testicles along a tube leading to the penis. On the way, they mix with a liquid called semen that gives them energy to swim. In sexual intercourse, sperm cells are released into the vagina by the penis. The sperm swim into the womb and from there to the oviducts. Egg cells made in the ovaries are also released into the oviducts, where they meet the sperm cells.

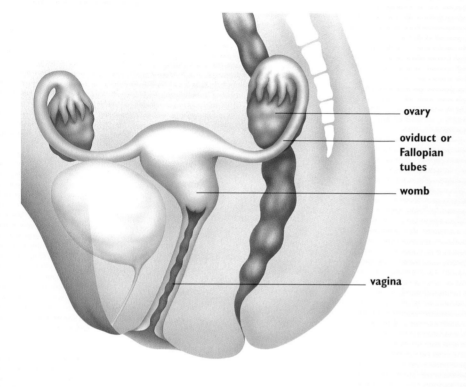

ovary

oviduct or Fallopian tubes

womb

vagina

bladder

penis

prostate gland

testicle

FERTILIZATION

When a sperm cell and egg cell meet, the two nuclei fuse (join) to form the zygote. This process is called fertilization.

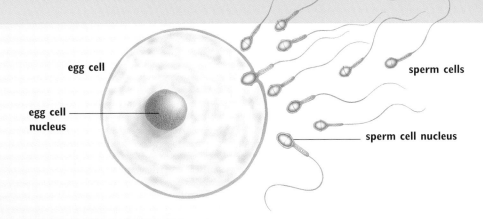

egg cell

egg cell nucleus

sperm cells

sperm cell nucleus

A bag of liquid called the amniotic fluid develops around the fetus to protect it while it is in the womb.

IN THE WOMB

The newly formed zygote divides several times to form a ball of cells. This then moves from the oviduct into the womb, where it attaches itself to the wall. One part of the ball forms the fetus (the developing baby). The other part forms an organ called the placenta. The placenta receives nutrients and oxygen from the mother's blood and passes them to the fetus. It also receives wastes from the fetus and passes them into the mother's blood.

HOW DOES AMNIOTIC FLUID PROTECT THE FETUS?

Make a clay model of a baby. Put it in a plastic bag (the womb), and tie it shut with some air trapped inside. Shake the bag—what happens to the baby? Now fill the bag with water and close it again. What happens when you shake the bag now?

GABRIEL FALLOPIUS

Gabriel Fallopius (1523–1562) was an Italian scientist taught by Vesalius (see page 17). He went on to make dissections and discoveries of his own. He was the first to identify the tubes (oviducts) connecting the ovaries to the womb. In honor of his discovery, the oviducts are often called Fallopian tubes.

MICROBES AND DISEASE

Tiny organisms called microorganisms, or microbes, can invade the body. When they do, they can cause disease. There are four kinds of microbes—bacteria, viruses, fungi, and protists.

BACTERIA

Bacteria are even smaller than human cells. Many kinds of bacteria live on the outside of the body and in the digestive tract without causing us any harm. Some even help to break down food. However, a few types of bacteria can cause serious diseases such as cholera, typhoid, and tuberculosis.

Different bacteria have distinctive shapes. Some are rod-shaped; others are rounded. These bacteria have long, whip-like hairs that they use to move.

TOOTH DECAY

Investigations on bacteria in the mouth have shown that some feed on sugar in foods and make acids, which cause tooth decay. Sweet snacks contain large amounts of sugar that the bacteria can feed on. By switching to snacks low in sugar, such as raw carrots or celery, people can reduce their chances of tooth decay.

These tiny structures are viruses exploding from an infected cell. They can breed rapidly in a body, causing disease and sometimes death.

VIRUSES

Viruses are even smaller than bacteria: they can be seen only by using a powerful electron microscope. Viruses cause diseases such as the common cold, influenza, and chickenpox. Viruses are made of an outer layer of protein and an inner core of DNA (the genetic material of living things). Viruses cannot grow or reproduce on their own. They must infect another living cell and take control. The virus puts the cell's machinery to work making copies of itself. Eventually, the cell bursts and releases thousands more viruses.

24

FUNGI

Fungi are less common on the body than bacteria and viruses. However, some kinds can settle on damp skin and feed on it. Gym locker rooms and swimming pools are places where a person may pick up a disease called athlete's foot. This is caused by a fungus and produces cracked and sore skin between the toes.

CHECKING FOR SPORES

Fungi produce tiny "seeds" called spores, which can travel on the gentlest of air currents. See if there are any fungal spores in the air in your room. Leave a slice of damp bread in your room for an hour, then seal it in a plastic bag. Check the bread every day for a few days. If there were fungal spores in the air, mold will form on the bread.

PROTISTS

Most protists have a body made from a single cell and live either in fresh water or in the sea. A few are parasites that live in people or animals. Some, such as the parasite that causes malaria, live part of their life in one organism and part of their life in another.

The microscope helped Pasteur show that some diseases were caused by microbes.

Louis Pasteur (1822–1895) was a French scientist who investigated substances such as wine and broth to find out why they went bad. Looking at them under a microscope, he found that it was due to the presence of microbes. He suggested that diseases were caused by microbes and that some may be passed from one person to another through coughs, sneezes, or touch. Later work by other scientists showed that Pasteur's ideas were correct.

Malaria parasites live in mosquitoes and humans. They invade human red blood cells and destroy them, as this magnified image shows.

FIGHTING DISEASE

The body has a variety of defenses against any microbes that try to invade it. Together, they make up the immune system. Sometimes microbes break through the defenses and cause disease, but even then the body may eventually destroy the microbes and return to full health. Medicines and vaccines have been developed to help and to give extra protection.

LINES OF DEFENSE

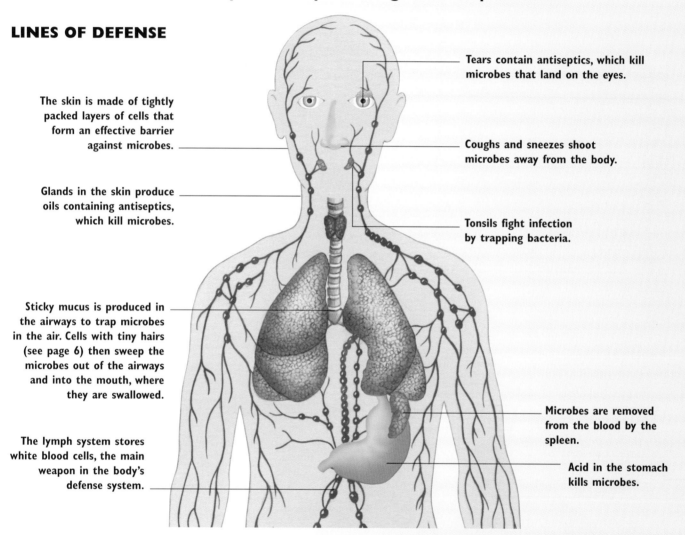

Tears contain antiseptics, which kill microbes that land on the eyes.

The skin is made of tightly packed layers of cells that form an effective barrier against microbes.

Glands in the skin produce oils containing antiseptics, which kill microbes.

Coughs and sneezes shoot microbes away from the body.

Tonsils fight infection by trapping bacteria.

Sticky mucus is produced in the airways to trap microbes in the air. Cells with tiny hairs (see page 6) then sweep the microbes out of the airways and into the mouth, where they are swallowed.

Microbes are removed from the blood by the spleen.

The lymph system stores white blood cells, the main weapon in the body's defense system.

Acid in the stomach kills microbes.

WHITE BLOOD CELLS

If microbes get past the body's first lines of defense and into the blood, they are attacked by white blood cells. Some white blood cells can engulf, or swallow, microbes. Other white cells produce antibodies. These are substances that attach to microbes and make them stick together. They can then be engulfed by white blood cells. There are many different antibodies. Each one is effective against a particular type of microbe.

MEDICINES

Medicines have been developed to defend the body against all kinds of microbe attacks. Antiseptic creams are used to kill microbes of all kinds around cuts. There are also many drugs that work against microbes, such as antibiotics (drugs that kill bacteria), antiviral agents, and antifungal drugs.

VACCINES

Vaccines are used to make the body safe from the attack of certain microbes. A vaccine contains dead or weakened microbes or the poisons they make. The body reacts to an injection of these substances by making antibodies, which can attack the live microbes if they enter the body. This prevents the disease from developing.

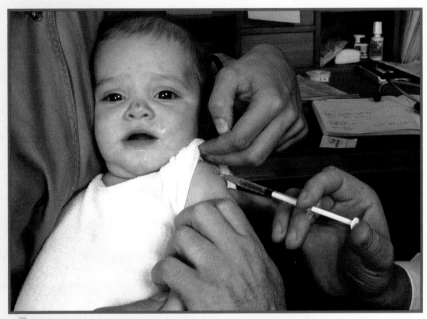

This vaccine will give protection against a deadly disease.

Alexander Fleming (1881–1955), a Scottish scientist, was studying bacteria by growing them on dishes of jelly when an accident happened. A spore of fungus landed on a dish of jelly, and the fungus began to grow. Fleming noticed that the bacteria on the jelly around the fungus died. He thought that the fungus was producing a substance that killed the bacteria. When he performed investigations to test his idea, he found that it was correct. From Fleming's work, antibiotics such as penicillin have been developed to fight many diseases caused by bacteria.

DISCOVERING **VACCINES**

An English doctor named Edward Jenner (1749–1823) noticed that milkmaids seemed to be immune to smallpox. He then discovered that the milkmaids caught a much milder disease, cowpox, from the cows that they milked. Jenner thought that the milkmaids were immune to smallpox because they had had cowpox. To test this idea, he vaccinated a boy named James Phipps with cowpox germs, then vaccinated him with smallpox germs. The boy did not get smallpox—he had become immune. Jenner's work led to the development of vaccines against diseases such as mumps, measles, and polio and the virtual eradication of smallpox.

Contemporary drawing of Edward Jenner vaccinating eight-year-old James Phipps.

STAYING HEALTHY

Today, we know an enormous amount about the human body. For instance, we understand that our bodies are made up of billions of tiny cells. We know that our skeleton holds us up, our muscles make us move, our nerves carry messages, and our digestive system breaks down food. Doctors have learned that microbes cause many diseases. We have drugs to help cure some diseases, and vaccines to prevent others.

PREVENTING ILLNESS

Doctors today use their knowledge of the human body to help prevent illness. For instance, doctors can help reduce patients' chances of getting heart disease by giving them regular checkups and getting them to change their lifestyle. Medical research has shown that regular exercise and cutting down on fatty foods are both ways of helping prevent heart disease.

This doctor is checking a patient's blood pressure. High blood pressure can indicate heart disease and various other illnesses.

CURING DISEASE

Medical research has greatly improved the treatment of many diseases. For instance, many cancer sufferers today have a much better chance of survival than they did 30 years ago. Regular checkups mean that cancers are now detected much earlier, before they become impossible to stop. Another area in which research is important is the treatment of asthma. In recent years, there has been a great increase in the number of sufferers, leading to more investigations into the causes of asthma and how it can be controlled.

This boy suffers from asthma. He is using an inhaler to prevent an attack. Scientific research is continuing to improve our understanding of this condition.

IS YOUR LIFESTYLE HEALTHY?

To keep healthy, you should do some form of exercise every day and eat a balanced diet (see page 9). You should also get plenty of sleep, which gives your body the chance to renew and repair itself, and brush your teeth twice a day.

Keep a diary of your lifestyle for a week—does it match the suggestions made here?

MAPPING OUR GENES

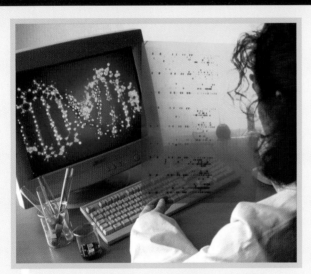

Genes are made from a substance called DNA. This scientist is looking at a model of the DNA molecule on a computer.

In 2000, scientists announced that they had mapped the entire human genome —all the **DNA** in a human cell. The DNA carries a coded set of instructions for producing a human being.

Although scientists know what all the genes look like, they do not yet know what most of them do. If they can find out, they may find the causes of many illnesses, and why our bodies begin to break down as we get older.

The way that leeches were used in the past probably did people more harm than good. However, today doctors are using leeches once again, to control swelling during plastic surgery.

The ancient Greeks believed that the body contained four fluids called humors. The humors were blood, phlegm, yellow bile, and black bile. Blood was thought to be hot, and too much of it caused fever. Phlegm was cold, and too much caused colds. Yellow bile was dry, and too much caused coughing. Black bile was moist, and it could make people feel sad or depressed. The Greeks believed that diseases developed if the four humors were not in balance. This idea was believed by doctors for more than 2,000 years, and they often used leeches to treat patients suffering from fever. This was done to draw out blood and restore the balance. It wasn't until much later that the work of Lind (page 9) and Pasteur (page 25) found that diet and microbes were the real cause of many diseases.

TIMELINE

Claudius Galen (A.D. 129–216), a Greek doctor, dissected animals and believed that the insides of the human body were arranged in the same way.

Andreas Vesalius (1514–1564), a Flemish (Belgian) scientist, dissected human bodies and showed that Galen was wrong to think the insides of humans and animals were the same.

Gabriel Fallopius (1523–1562), an Italian scientist, made dissections of the human body and discovered that the ovaries in females were connected to the womb by tubes. They were named Fallopian tubes.

William Harvey (1578–1657), an English surgeon, discovered that the heart pumps blood around the body.

James Lind (1716–1794), a Scottish doctor, discovered that including citrus fruits in a person's diet could prevent scurvy.

Edward Jenner (1749–1823), an English doctor, discovered that vaccination can protect the body from disease.

Rene Laennec (1781–1826), a French doctor, invented the stethoscope, which enabled doctors to listen to the heart and lungs more effectively.

William Beaumont (1785–1853), an American surgeon, investigated digestion by placing food through a hole in the stomach wall of one of his patients.

John Snow (1813–1858), an English doctor, showed that cholera could be spread by people drinking polluted water.

Crawford Long (1815–1878), an American doctor, used ether as an anesthetic in an operation in 1842. This was the first time that an anesthetic had been used in surgery.

Louis Pasteur (1822–1895), a French scientist, suggested that some microbes may cause disease.

Joseph Lister (1827–1912), an English surgeon, used carbolic acid as an antiseptic during surgery and found that it helped his patients to recover.

William Perkin (1838–1907), an English chemist, made dyes from substances in coal tar.

Robert Koch (1843–1910), a German scientist, discovered that cholera was caused by a bacterium, or kind of microbe.

Wilhelm Roentgen (1845–1923), a German physicist, discovered X rays in 1895. In 1896, he showed that they could be used to see the bones in the hand. X rays have been used to examine the inside of the body ever since.

Paul Ehrlich (1854–1915), a German scientist, used dyes to see the structure of cells more clearly under a microscope.

Hans Berger (1873–1941), a German scientist, recorded the electrical activity of the brain with a device called an electroencephalogram (EEG).

Alexander Fleming (1881–1955), a Scottish scientist, conducted investigations that led to the discovery of antibiotics.

GLOSSARY

antibiotics – chemicals developed to kill bacteria that cause disease. Some micro-organisms produce antibiotics.

bacteria – very small, single-celled living things (microbes) in which the DNA is not contained in a nucleus. They can cause disease.

cartilage – a tough substance with a smooth surface that protects the joints in the body.

cell – a tiny packet of jelly-like cytoplasm enclosed in a thin membrane. Most cells have a nucleus containing DNA. The simplest life-forms are single cells, but more complicated plants and animals are formed from millions of cells.

diagnose – to identify the cause of an illness by examining a patient and finding out his or her symptoms.

electrode – a wire that can conduct electricity.

enzyme – a chemical made by a cell that helps life processes such as digestion and respiration happen faster.

fungi – living things such as mushrooms and molds. Many fungi are microbes, and they feed on dead or living plants and animals. They reproduce by making large numbers of spores.

hormone – a chemical produced by organs in the body called glands. Hormones travel in the blood and affect the activity of various parts of the body.

immune – safe from catching something, such as a disease.

minerals – simple chemicals found in soil that plants need for healthy growth. Humans also need minerals such as calcium (which helps build strong bones) in their diet.

nutrients – substances in food that the body needs for energy, growth, and good health.

ovaries – the organs in a female's body where the eggs are made.

parasite – an animal or plant that lives on or in the body of another living thing and gets its food from it. Some parasites cause disease.

protein – an important nutrient that supplies materials for growth and repair of the body.

protists – microscopic living things (microbes) with bodies made from just a single cell. They may feed like animals or make food using light like plants.

respiration – the process of releasing energy from food to the cells in the body by taking oxygen into the blood and giving out carbon dioxide. This takes place when a living thing breathes.

spores – thousands of tiny "seeds" produced by a fungus. New fungi grow from the spores.

testicles – the organs in a male's body that make sperm cells.

vaccine – a substance used to stimulate the body to protect itself from a disease.

viruses – tiny organisms that do not have a cell structure. When they are introduced into a body, they reproduce in its cells and cause tissue damage and disease.

INDEX